Bones, Bones, Dinosaur Bones

by Byron Barton

HarperCollins*Publishers*

Bones, Bones, Dinosaur Bones. Copyright © 1990 by Byron Barton. Manufactured in Vietnam. All rights reserved. For information address HarperCollins Children's Books,
a division of HarperCollins Publishers, 195 Broadway, New York, NY 10007. 23 SCP 31 Library of Congress Cataloging-in-Publication
Data. Barton, Byron. Bones, bones, dinosaur bones / Byron Barton.   p.   cm.   Summary: A cast of characters looks for, finds, and assembles some dinosaur bones.
ISBN 0-690-04825-4. — ISBN 0-690-04827-0 (lib. bdg.)   (1. Dinosaurs—Fiction.)   I. Title.   PZ7.B2848Bo   1990(E)—dc20   89-71306   CIP   AC

Bones. Bones. We look for bones.

Tyrannosaurus, Apatosaurus, Stegosaurus, Ankylosaurus, Parasaurolophus, Gallimimus, Thecodontosaurus, Triceratops.

We look for the bones of dinosaurs.

We find them.

We dig them up.

We wrap them

and pack them.

We load them on trucks.

We have the bones of dinosaurs.

We have head bones, foot bones, leg bones,

rib bones, back bones, teeth and claws.

We put the claws on the foot bones

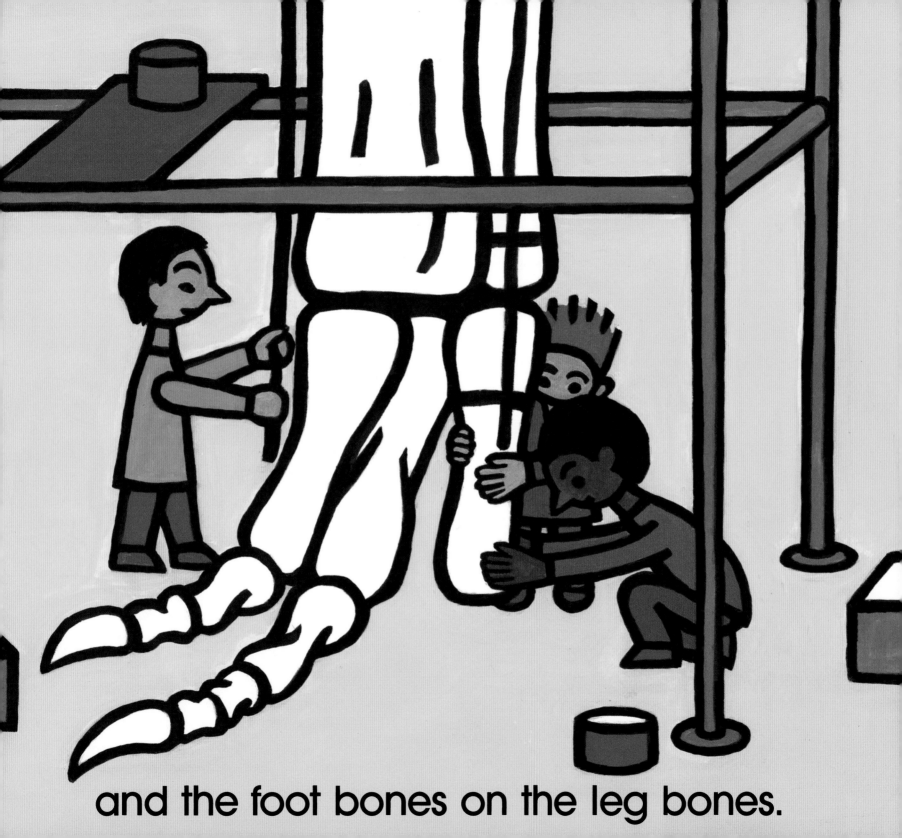

and the foot bones on the leg bones.

We put the teeth in the head bones

and the head bones on the neck bones.

We put the rib bones on the back bones.

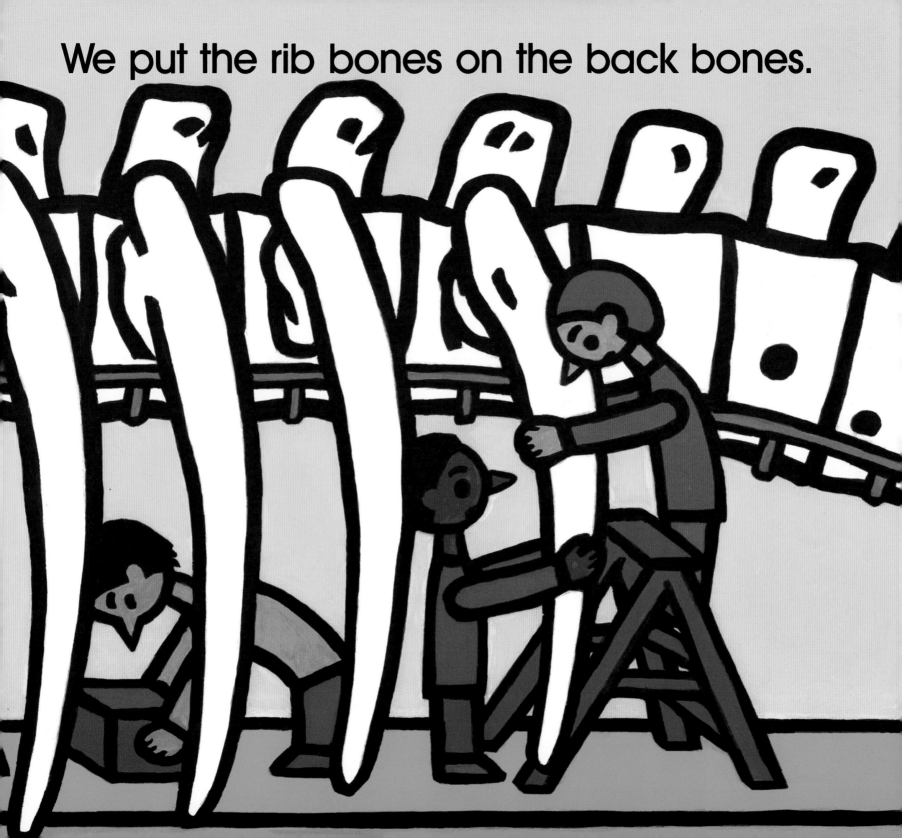

And the tail bones are last.

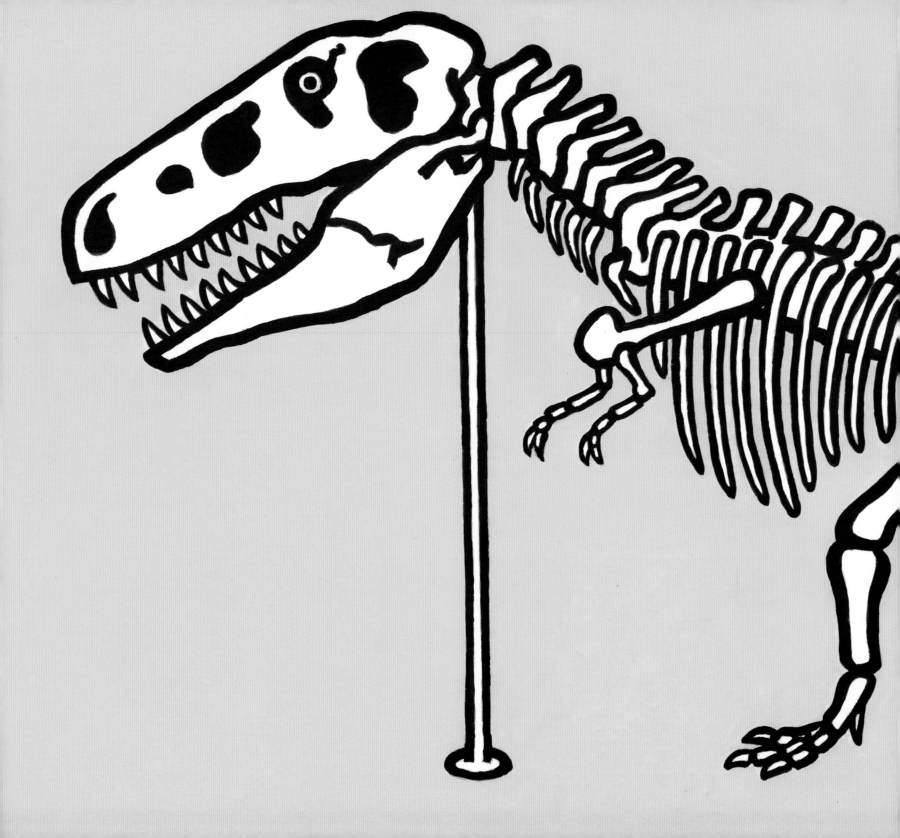

These are the bones of Tyrannosaurus rex.

Bones. Bones. We look for bones.

Apatosaurus
(ah-PAT-oh-SAW-rus)

Gallimimus
(gal-li-MY-mus)

STEGOSAURUS
(steg-oh-SAW-rus)

Parasaurolophus
(PARE-ah-saw-ROH-lah-fus)

Tyrannosaurus rex
(ty-ran-oh-SAW-rus rex)

Ankylosaurus
(an-KY-loh-SAW-rus)

Thicodontosaurus
(thee-coh-don-toh-SAW-rus)

Triceratops
(try-SARE-ah-TOPS)

We look for the bones of dinosaurs.